I0805246

JOAN TOWER

FANFARE FOR THE UNCOMMON WOMAN No. 5

Trumpet Quartet

(Score and Parts)

AMP 8122
First Printing: December 1997

ISBN 978-0-7935-7874-0

Associated Music Publishers, Inc.

DISTRIBUTED BY
HAL•LEONARD®
CORPORATION
7777 W. BLUEMOUND RD. P.O. BOX 13819 MILWAUKEE, WI 53213

Fanfare for the Uncommon Woman, No. 5, was commissioned by the Aspen Music Festival for the opening of the Joan and Irving Harris Concert Hall on August 20, 1993.

The trumpets should be positioned as far apart as possible, in pairs. The *Fanfare* may also be played with multiple trumpets doubling on each part, soloing where necessary.

The work is dedicated, with affection, to Joan Harris.

—Joan Tower

duration: ca. 3 minutes

to Joan Harris

FANFARE FOR THE UNCOMMON WOMAN
No. 5

Joan Tower
(1993)

22
mf poco marcato
pp
mf poco marcato
mf poco marcato
27
mf
mf
mf
mf
32
cresc.
cresc.
f
cresc.
cresc.
f
f
f
f

Trumpet 1 in C

to Joan Harris

FANFARE FOR THE UNCOMMON WOMAN
No. 5

Joan Tower
(1993)

accel. molto
♩ = ca. 132
open
Poco più mosso
marc.
cresc.

Trumpet 2 in C

to Joan Harris

FANFARE FOR THE UNCOMMON WOMAN
No. 5

Joan Tower
(1993)

accel. molto
♩ = ca. 132
open
Poco più mosso
marc.
marc.
cresc.

Trumpet 3 in C

to Joan Harris

FANFARE FOR THE UNCOMMON WOMAN
No. 5

Joan Tower
(1993)

62
open
mf
mfp
mf cresc.
68
f
72
mf
mfp
mf
78
f
83
Poco più mosso
f
89
mf
f
94
mf marc. cresc.
ff
98
ff
ff
103
fp
fp
108
mp
ff
ffp
ff

to Joan Harris

Trumpet 4 in C

FANFARE FOR THE UNCOMMON WOMAN
No. 5

Joan Tower
(1993)

open
Poco più mosso
f marc.
cresc.
marc.

36
mf
f
mf
40
broaden
Poco meno mosso (♩ = ca. 104)
dim.
mp
dolce
f
p
45
rit.
♩ = ca. 100
mute (cup)
pp dolce
mute (cup)
pp dolce
mute (cup)
pp dolce
mute (cup)
dim.
pp
pp
dolce

accel. molto
open
open
♩ = ca. 132
open
open
cresc.

68
72
77

Poco più mosso
82
f
f marc.
f
mf
86
mf
f marc.
f
f
mf
f marc.
92
cresc.
mf marc.
cresc.
f
mf marc.
cresc.
mf
cresc.
marc.

96
100
107